At Home

by Max Park

PEARSON

Glenview, Illinois • Boston, Massachusetts
Chandler, Arizona • Upper Saddle River, New Jersey

We are at home.
What do we see?

We see coats.

We see toys.
We play.

We see a room.
What is in the room?

We see clothes.

We see a sink.

A family eats at home.
What is at your home?